Dr Michael M. Grunebe...
designer and writer of the ...
Language Courses, is wide...
international expert on memory improvement. A
Senior Lecturer in Psychology at University College,
Swansea, he has published a large number of
articles in scientific journals, as well as a number of
well-known books on the application of memory
research. He has also lectured widely in both the UK
and the USA and given keynote addresses to several
international scientific conferences. In 1988 he
provided the original script for, and appeared in, *The
Magic of Memory*, a programme in the BBC
television QED series which illustrated many
memory techniques, including his own Linkword
Method, and he recently acted as principal scientific
consultant for a major BBC 1 series on memory.

Since it was first published in 1987, the Linkword
system has been both highly successful and widely
acclaimed and Linkword books are now published
throughout the world. Dr Gruneberg works with
highly qualified language experts to produce
Linkword books which teach you not only **what** to
learn, but **how to remember what you have
learned**, more quickly and more enjoyably than you
ever imagined!

Gabriel C. Jacobs BA, PhD,
the language consultant for this book, is a Senior
Lecturer in the School of European Languages at
Swansea University. He has been involved for some
time in the practical application of language.

Also by Dr Michael M. Gruneberg

LINKWORD LANGUAGE SYSTEM: FRENCH
LINKWORD LANGUAGE SYSTEM: FURTHER FRENCH

LINKWORD: SPANISH IN A DAY
LINKWORD LANGUAGE SYSTEM: SPANISH
LINKWORD LANGUAGE SYSTEM: GERMAN
LINKWORD LANGUAGE SYSTEM: ITALIAN
LINKWORD LANGUAGE SYSTEM: GREEK
LINKWORD LANGUAGE SYSTEM: PORTUGUESE
(with Dr G. C. Jacobs)

and published by Corgi Books

LINKWORD

FRENCH
IN A DAY

Dr Michael M. Gruneberg

Language Consultant
Dr Gabriel C. Jacobs

CORGI BOOKS

LINKWORD: FRENCH IN A DAY

A CORGI BOOK : 0 552 14246 8

First publication in Great Britain

PRINTING HISTORY
Corgi edition published 1994

Set in 9pt Linotype New Century Schoolbook by
Phoenix Typesetting, Ilkley, West Yorkshire.

Corgi Books are published by Transworld Publishers Ltd,
61–63 Uxbridge Road, Ealing, London W5 5SA,
in Australia by Transworld Publishers (Australia) Pty Ltd,
15–25 Helles Avenue, Moorebank, NSW 2170,
and in New Zealand by Transworld Publishers (NZ) Ltd,
3 William Pickering Drive, Albany, Auckland.

Reproduced, printed and bound in Great Britain by
Cox & Wyman Ltd, Reading, Berks.

Contents

Foreword

This book is designed to get you to pick up, **in a single day,** an extensive targeted vocabulary which will enable you to communicate in useful situations you are likely to meet in France, such as in the restaurant, at the hotel, travelling, shopping, in emergencies and so on. It is ideal, therefore, if you have to be in France tomorrow or next week on holiday or business, or for the student who wants to acquire an extensive vocabulary rapidly. You can even learn a useful amount on the plane!

Why then is learning so quick and easy? Because Linkword courses are unique in **not only teaching you what to learn, but how to remember what you learn.** This is done through the use of images which make you link the English word to another word which sounds like the French word you want to remember. For example, the French word for Tablecloth is Nappe. You are asked to picture yourself having a **nap** on a tablecloth.

Over fifty studies published in scientific journals have shown this method to be far superior to ordinary methods of learning. In one study the number of foreign words remembered increased from 28% to 88% using this method. What is more, the method works for those who are good at language learning and those who are poor at it. Even more important, a number of studies show that the great majority of people find it more **fun** learning this way.

This book concentrates on teaching useful nouns, although other helpful words are included. This is because if you are beginning a language nouns are all-important for communication. If you are in a restaurant for example, and can say 'Bill please!', you will be presented with the bill. If you just say 'I want' you won't get anything! You will be amazed at how much difference a knowledge of the contents of this book will make to your enjoyment of your holiday or trip abroad and to overcoming the feeling of isolation you often get when you don't understand the language of the country you are visiting. Anyone who has ever used a phrase book will know how difficult they are to use, and how useful it is to know the words one needs, instead of trying to look them up. This book allows you to be your own mental phrase book!

When you have finished this book you can go on to learn even more French by using Linkword French, a more advanced French language course, and its accompanying audio tape which will help to improve your pronunciation.

How to use Linkword

1] You will be presented with words like this:
The French for TABLECLOTH is NAPPE
Imagine having a NAP on a TABLECLOTH
What you do is to imagine this picture in your mind's eye as vividly as possible.

2] After you have read the image you should think about it in your mind's eye for about 10 seconds before moving on to the next word. If you do not spend enough time thinking about the image it will not stick in your memory as well as it should.

3] Sometimes the word in French and in English is the same or very similar. For example, the French for 'taxi' is 'taxi'. When this happens you will be asked to associate the word in some way with the Eiffel Tower.

For example:
Imagine a taxi driving under the Eiffel Tower.
Whenever the Eiffel Tower comes to mind, therefore, you will know the word is the same or similar in both English and French.

4] **PRONUNCIATION**
The approximate pronunciation of words is given in brackets after the word is presented for the first time.

For example:
The French for CABBAGE is CHOU (SHOO)
(SHOO) is the way the word is pronounced.

When the following letters appear, in the words in brackets (pronunciation words) they sound like this:

'j' sounds like the 'S' in pleasure.
'oo' sounds like a sort of 'OO' sound.
'n' sounds like the 'N' in fiancé.
'e' sounds like the 'U' in curl.

For example:

The French for garage is garage (GARAJ).
The French for skirt is jupe (JooP).
The French for rabbit is lapin (LAPAHn).
The French for the is le (Le).

Don't worry too much about these pronunciations to begin with. The approximate pronunciation given in brackets will allow you to be understood.

5] **ACCENTS**

As accents can often be omitted on capital letters in French, there are no accents in this course. This has been done to help you learn quickly. However the correct accents are given in the glossary at the end of the book.

IMPORTANT NOTES

Don't worry if you don't get all the words correct the first time you go through the book. No-one can expect to get all the words right first time. Don't worry about what you can't remember, think of all the words you do remember! Only after you have reached the end of the book should you go back to learn any words you have forgotten.

You can carry on learning until you feel tired. However, if you begin to feel tired, you must stop and take a break.

FOOD AND DRINK WORDS

THINK OF EACH IMAGE IN YOUR MIND'S EYE FOR ABOUT TEN SECONDS. FOR EXAMPLE, THE FRENCH FOR *CABBAGE* IS *CHOU*, (PRONOUNCED SHOO), IMAGINE IN YOUR MIND'S EYE A *CABBAGE* GROWING OUT OF A *SHOE*.

NOTE: THE WORD IN BRACKETS ON THE RIGHT HAND SIDE OF THE PAGE IS THE WAY THE WORD IS PRONOUNCED.

○ The French for CABBAGE is CHOU   (SHOO)
Imagine a cabbage growing out of a SHOE.

○ The French for POTATO is POMME DE   (POM De TER)
TERRE
Imagine Australians throwing potatoes at
Englishmen ('Poms') trying to land in
Australia – the potatoes are POM DETERRents.

○ The French for TOMATO is TOMATE   (TOMAT)
Imagine throwing TOMATOES at the Eiffel Tower.
* Remember whenever the Eiffel Tower is given in an image
the word is the same or similar in English and French.

○ The French for EGG is OEUF   (eF)
Imagine telling a chicken to get OFF her egg.

○ The French for BUTTER is BEURRE   (BeR)
Imagine you hear a cat PURR after it has
eaten some butter.
* Remember the 'e' sounds like the 'U' in curl.

○ The French for BREAD is PAIN   (PAHn)
Imagine putting loaves of bread in a PAN.
* Remember the 'n' sounds like the 'N' in fiancé.

○ The French for MILK is LAIT   (LAY)
Imagine a hen which LAYS a bottle of milk.

○ The French for WATER is EAU   (OH)
Imagine that you OWE a mean Frenchman
for a glass of water.

YOU CAN WRITE YOUR ANSWERS IN, BUT COVER UP THE
RIGHT-HAND PAGE BEFORE GIVING YOUR ANSWERS

O   What is the English for EAU? (OH)   _____

O   What is the English for LAIT? (LAY)   _____

O   What is the English for PAIN? (PAHn)   _____

O   What is the English for BEURRE? (BeR)   _____

O   What is the English for OEUF? (eF)   _____

O   What is the English for TOMATE?
     (TOMAT)   _____

O   What is the English for POMME DE
     TERRE? (POM De TER)   _____

O   What is the English for CHOU? (SHOO)   _____

TURN BACK FOR THE ANSWERS

YOU CAN WRITE YOUR ANSWERS IN, BUT COVER UP THE LEFT-HAND PAGE BEFORE GIVING YOUR ANSWERS

○   What is the French for water?   _____

○   What is the French for milk?   _____

○   What is the French for bread?   _____

○   What is the French for butter?   _____

○   What is the French for egg?   _____

○   What is the French for tomato?   _____

○   What is the French for potato?   _____

○   What is the French for cabbage?   _____

TURN BACK FOR THE ANSWERS

RESTAURANT WORDS

THINK OF EACH IMAGE IN YOUR MIND'S EYE FOR ABOUT TEN SECONDS

○ The French for CUTLERY is COUVERT   (KOOVER)
  Imagine that you COVER up the cutlery.

○ The French for TABLECLOTH is NAPPE   (NAP)
  Imagine taking a NAP on a tablecloth.

○ The French for GLASS is VERRE   (VER)
  Imagine telling the waiter that it is not
  FAIR that you don't have a glass.

○ The French for DRINK is BOISSON   (BWASOHn)
  Imagine pouring your drink into a BASIN.

○ The French for FOOD is NOURRITURE   (NOOREETooR)
  Imagine asking the waiter if there is food to
  NOURISH YOUR body.

○ The French for DINNER is DINER   (DEENAY)
  Imagine having DINNER in the Eiffel Tower.

○ The French for MEAT is VIANDE   (VEE OnD)
  Imagine a German waiter saying 'VE
  HAND the meat to you.'

○ The French for TIP is POURBOIRE   (POORBWAR)
  Imagine thinking 'This is a POOR BAR. I
  won't leave a tip.'

YOU CAN WRITE YOUR ANSWERS IN, BUT COVER UP THE
LEFT-HAND PAGE BEFORE GIVING YOUR ANSWERS

O   What is the English for POURBOIRE?
     (POORBWAR)   _____

O   What is the English for VIANDE?
     (VEE OnD)   _____

O   What is the English for DINER?
     (DEENAY)   _____

O   What is the English for NOURRITURE?
     (NOOREETooR)   _____

O   What is the English for BOISSON?
     (BWASOHn)   _____

O   What is the English for VERRE? (VER)   _____

O   What is the English for NAPPE? (NAP)   _____

O   What is the English for COUVERT?
     (KOOVER)   _____

YOU CAN WRITE YOUR ANSWERS IN

○   What is the French for tip?   _____

○   What is the French for meat?   _____

○   What is the French for dinner?   _____

○   What is the French for food?   _____

○   What is the French for drink?   _____

○   What is the French for glass?   _____

○   What is the French for tablecloth?   _____

○   What is the French for cutlery?   _____

TURN BACK FOR THE ANSWERS

TRAVELLING, THE CAR

THINK OF EACH IMAGE IN YOUR MIND'S EYE FOR ABOUT TEN SECONDS

○ The French for PASSPORT is PASSEPORT   (PASPOR)
Imagine your PASSPORT has a picture of
the Eiffel Tower on the front.

○ The French for CUSTOMS is DOUANE   (DWAN)
Imagine going through customs counting
'D'ONE, D'two, D'three.'

○ The French for TOILET is TOILETTES   (TWALET)
Imagine a TOILET right at the top of the
Eiffel Tower.

○ The French for ENTRANCE is ENTREE   (OnTRAY)
Imagine making your entrance ON a TRAY.

○ The French for EXIT is SORTIE   (SORTEE)
Imagine having SORE TEETH after
bumping them at the exit of a cinema.

○ The French for SUITCASE is VALISE   (VALEEZ)
Imagine suitcases strewn all over the VALLEYS.

○ The French for TICKET is BILLET   (BEE AY)
Imagine buying a ticket for a BA (British
Airways) flight.

○ The French for MONEY is ARGENT   (ARJOn)
Imagine needing money to go to the ARGENTine.
(N.B. ARGENT is also the word for SILVER.)
* Remember the 'j' sounds like the 'S' in pleasure.

YOU CAN WRITE YOUR ANSWERS IN, BUT COVER UP THE
RIGHT-HAND PAGE BEFORE GIVING YOUR ANSWERS

O   What is the English for ARGENT?
    (ARJOn)   _____

O   What is the English for BILLET?
    (BEE AY)   _____

O   What is the English for VALISE?
    (VALEEZ)   _____

O   What is the English for SORTIE?
    (SORTEE)   _____

O   What is the English for ENTREE?
    (OnTRAY)   _____

O   What is the English for TOILETTES?
    (TWALET)   _____

O   What is the English for DOUANE?
    (DWAN)   _____

O   What is the English for PASSEPORT?
    (PASPOR)   _____

TURN BACK FOR THE ANSWERS

YOU CAN WRITE YOUR ANSWERS IN, BUT COVER UP THE LEFT-HAND PAGE BEFORE GIVING YOUR ANSWERS

○   What is the French for money?   _____

○   What is the French for ticket?   _____

○   What is the French for suitcase?   _____

○   What is the French for exit?   _____

○   What is the French for entrance?   _____

○   What is the French for toilet?   _____

○   What is the French for customs?   _____

○   What is the French for passport?   _____

TURN BACK FOR THE ANSWERS

CLOTHES

THINK OF EACH IMAGE IN YOUR MIND'S EYE FOR ABOUT TEN SECONDS

O   The French for UNDERPANTS is SLIP   (SLEEP)
Imagine you SLEEP in your underpants.

O   The French for TROUSERS is PANTALON   (POnTALOHn)
Imagine your trousers are baggy PANTALOONS.

O   The French for SKIRT is JUPE   (JooP)
Imagine spilling SOUP on your skirt.

O   The French for SOCK is CHAUSSETTE   (SHOSET)
Imagine you buy a magnificent pair of
socks – they are a SHOW SET.

O   The French for JACKET is VESTE   (VEST)
Imagine you wear a VEST while everybody
else is wearing a smart jacket to a dance.

O   The French for DRESS is ROBE   (ROB)
Imagine someone ROBS you of your best dress.

O   The French for SHOE is CHAUSSURE   (SHOSooR)
Imagine Geoffrey CHAUCER, the author of
The Canterbury Tales, trying on a shoe on his
way to Canterbury.

O   The French for HAT is CHAPEAU   (SHAPOH)
Imagine taking off your hat when you enter a
CHAPEL.

YOU CAN WRITE YOUR ANSWERS IN, BUT COVER UP THE
LEFT-HAND PAGE BEFORE GIVING YOUR ANSWERS

○   What is the English for CHAPEAU?
     (SHAPOH)   _____

○   What is the English for CHAUSSURE?
     (SHOSooR)   _____

○   What is the English for ROBE? (ROB)   _____

○   What is the English for VESTE? (VEST)   _____

○   What is the English for CHAUSSETTE?
     (SHOSET)   _____

○   What is the English for JUPE? (JooP)   _____

○   What is the English for PANTALON?
     (POnTALOHn)   _____

○   What is the English for SLIP? (SLEEP)   _____

YOU CAN WRITE YOUR ANSWERS IN

○   What is the French for hat?   _____

○   What is the French for shoe?   _____

○   What is the French for dress?   _____

○   What is the French for jacket?   _____

○   What is the French for sock?   _____

○   What is the French for skirt?   _____

○   What is the French for trousers?   _____

○   What is the French for underpants?   _____

TURN BACK FOR THE ANSWERS

EMERGENCY WORDS

THINK OF EACH IMAGE IN YOUR MIND'S EYE FOR ABOUT TEN SECONDS

○ The French for DANGER is DANGER (DOnJAY)
Imagine a notice on the Eiffel Tower:
'DANGER, do not lean over.'

○ The French for FIRE! is AU FEU! (OH Fe)
Imagine feeling AWFUL because you are
caught in a fire.

○ The French for AMBULANCE is (OnBooLOnS)
AMBULANCE.
Imagine AMBULANCES racing to the Eiffel Tower.

○ The French for HELP! is AU SECOURS! (OH SKOOR)
Imagine OSCAR Wilde shouting for help.

○ The French for HOSPITAL is HOPITAL (OPEETAL)
Imagine the Eiffel Tower converted into a HOSPITAL.

○ The French for TELEPHONE is (TAYLAYFON)
TELEPHONE
Imagine throwing TELEPHONES from the
top of the Eiffel Tower.

○ The French for DOCTOR is MEDECIN (MAYDSAHn)
Imagine a doctor giving you MEDICINE.

○ The French for DENTIST is DENTISTE (DOnTEEST)
Imagine a DENTIST taking your teeth out
in the Eiffel Tower.

YOU CAN WRITE YOUR ANSWERS IN, BUT COVER UP THE
RIGHT-HAND PAGE BEFORE GIVING YOUR ANSWERS

○   What is the English for DENTISTE?
    (DOnTEEST)   _____

○   What is the English for MEDECIN?
    (MAYDSAHn)   _____

○   What is the English for TELEPHONE?
    (TAYLAYFON)   _____

○   What is the English for HOPITAL?
    (OPEETAL)   _____

○   What is the English for AU SECOURS!?
    (OH SKOOR)   _____

○   What is the English for AMBULANCE?
    (OnBooLOnS)   _____

○   What is the English for AU FEU!? (OH Fe)   _____

○   What is the English for DANGER?
    (DOnJAY)   _____

TURN BACK FOR THE ANSWERS

YOU CAN WRITE YOUR ANSWERS IN, BUT COVER UP THE
LEFT-HAND PAGE BEFORE GIVING YOUR ANSWERS

○   What is the French for dentist?   _____

○   What is the French for doctor?   _____

○   What is the French for telephone?   _____

○   What is the French for hospital?   _____

○   What is the French for help! ?   _____

○   What is the French for fire?   _____

○   What is the French for ambulance?   _____

○   What is the French for danger?   _____

TURN BACK FOR THE ANSWERS

NOW TEST YOURSELF

What is the English for

1] POMME DE TERRE ....
   (POM De TER)
2] BEURRE (BeR)..
3] COUVERT (KOOVER)..................................
4] POURBOIRE (POORBWAR)......................
5] SORTIE (SORTEE) ....
6] BILLET (BEE AY)..
7] SLIP (SLEEP)..
8] CHAUSSETTE (SHOSET)...........................
9] AU FEU! (OH Fe)...
10] MEDECIN (MAYDSAHn)............................
11] LAIT (LAY) ....
12] VERRE (VER)...
13] ENTREE (On TRAY)....................................
14] JUPE (JooP)..
15] DENTISTE (DOnTEEST)............................

What is the French for

1] CABBAGE.................................
2] BREAD ....
3] TABLECLOTH.........................
4] MEAT ....
5] CUSTOMS...............................
6] SUITCASE ....
7] DRESS.....................................
8] HAT ....
9] DANGER..................................
10] TELEPHONE............................
11] EGG ....
12] DINNER...................................
13] TOILET ....
14] SHOE.......................................
15] HOSPITAL..............................

Do not worry about the spelling at this stage.

THE ANSWERS ARE ON PAGE 18

THE ANSWERS ARE

1] POTATO	1] CHOU
2 BUTTER	2] PAIN
3] CUTLERY	3] NAPPE
4] TIP	4] VIANDE
5] EXIT	5] DOUANE
6] TICKET	6] VALISE
7] UNDERPANTS	7] ROBE
8] SOCK	8] CHAPEAU
9] FIRE!	9] DANGER
10] DOCTOR	10] TELEPHONE
11] MILK	11] OEUF
12] GLASS	12] DINER
13] ENTRANCE	13] TOILETTES
14] SKIRT	14] CHAUSSURE
15] DENTIST	15] HOPITAL

Count yourself correct if the word *sounds* like the French word you are looking for. If you scored more than 15/30 you have now learned more than 20 words. If you managed to translate all the words, you can assume you have learned all the words given up till now, i.e. 40 words.

FURNITURE AND FITTINGS

THINK OF EACH IMAGE IN YOUR MIND'S EYE FOR ABOUT TEN SECONDS

O The French for TABLE is TABLE   (TABL)
Imagine throwing a TABLE from the top of the
Eiffel Tower.

O The French for CHAIR is CHAISE   (SHEZ)
Imagine you have SHARES in a chair.

O The French for CUPBOARD is PLACARD   (PLAKAR)
Imagine a PLACARD stuck to a cupboard.

O The French for WARDROBE is ARMOIRE   (ARMWAR)
Imagine your ARM WORN out by trying to
open a wardrobe door that is stuck.

O The French for CLOCK is PENDULE   (POnDooL)
Imagine a grandfather clock with a large PENDULUM.

O The French for BED is LIT   (LEE)
Imagine you LAY on a bed.

O The French for PIANO is PIANO   (PEE ANOH)
Imagine playing a PIANO at the top of the
Eiffel Tower.

O The French for CURTAIN is RIDEAU   (REEDOH)
Imagine having to RE-DO the curtains after
you have made a mess of them.

O The French for ARMCHAIR is FAUTEUIL   (FOTOEY)
Imagine taking a PHOTO of an armchair.

O The French for CARPET is TAPIS   (TAPEE)
Imagine your carpet with a TAPESTRY border.

YOU CAN WRITE YOUR ANSWERS IN, BUT COVER UP THE
RIGHT-HAND PAGE BEFORE GIVING YOUR ANSWERS

O   What is the English for TAPIS? (TAPEE)   _____

O   What is the English for FAUTEUIL?
     (FOTOEY)   _____

O   What is the English for RIDEAU?
     (REEDOH)   _____

O   What is the English for PIANO?
     (PEE ANOH)   _____

O   What is the English for LIT? (LEE)   _____

O   What is the English for PENDULE?
     (POnDooL)   _____

O   What is the English for ARMOIRE?
     (ARMWAR)   _____

O   What is the English for PLACARD?
     (PLAKAR)   _____

O   What is the English for CHAISE? (SHEZ)   _____

O   What is the English for TABLE? (TABL)   _____

TURN BACK FOR THE ANSWERS

YOU CAN WRITE YOUR ANSWERS IN, BUT COVER UP THE
LEFT-HAND PAGE BEFORE GIVING YOUR ANSWERS

O   What is the French for carpet?   _____

O   What is the French for armchair?   _____

O   What is the French for curtain?   _____

O   What is the French for piano?   _____

O   What is the French for bed?   _____

O   What is the French for clock?   _____

O   What is the French for wardrobe?   _____

O   What is the French for cupboard?   _____

O   What is the French for chair?   _____

O   What is the French for table?   _____

TURN BACK FOR THE ANSWERS

MORE FOOD AND DRINK WORDS

THINK OF EACH IMAGE IN YOUR MIND'S EYE FOR ABOUT TEN SECONDS

○ The French for BEER is BIERE   (BEE ER)
Imagine pouring BEER from the top of the
Eiffel Tower.

○ The French for WINE is VIN   (VAHn)
Imagine a VAN delivering bottles of wine.

○ The French for APPLE is POMME   (POM)
Imagine someone who has an apple on
his head instead of a POM-POM.

○ The French for PEAR is POIRE   (PWAR)
Imagine being so POOR you can only
afford cheap pears.

○ The French for PEACH is PECHE   (PESH)
Imagine a child being a PEST until you
give him a peach.

○ The French for COFFEE is CAFE   (KAFAY)
Imagine drinking coffee in a French CAFE.

○ The French for CHEESE is FROMAGE   (FROMAJ)
Imagine someone who can't tell cheese
FROM MARGarine.

○ The French for MUSHROOM is   (SHOnPEENYOHn)
CHAMPIGNON
Imagine you have raised a CHAMPION
mushroom.

○ The French for GARLIC is AIL   (A EE)
Imagine someone poking you in the
EYE with a piece of garlic.

○ The French for SNAIL is ESCARGOT   (ESKARGOH)
Imagine a ship with ITS CARGO of snails.

YOU CAN WRITE YOUR ANSWERS IN, BUT COVER UP THE
LEFT-HAND PAGE BEFORE GIVING YOUR ANSWERS

O   What is the English for ESCARGOT?
(ESKARGOH)   _____

O   What is the English for AIL? (A EE)   _____

O   What is the English for CHAMPIGNON?
(SHOnPEENYOHn)   _____

O   What is the English for FROMAGE?
(FROMAJ)   _____

O   What is the English for CAFE? (KAFAY) _____

O   What is the English for PECHE? (PESH) _____

O   What is the English for POIRE? (PWAR) _____

O   What is the English for POMME? (POM) _____

O   What is the English for VIN? (VAHn)   _____

O   What is the English for BIERE? (BEE ER) _____

YOU CAN WRITE YOUR ANSWERS IN

O   What is the French for snail?   _____

O   What is the French for garlic?   _____

O   What is the French for mushroom?   _____

O   What is the French for cheese?   _____

O   What is the French for coffee?   _____

O   What is the French for peach?   _____

O   What is the French for pear?   _____

O   What is the French for apple?   _____

O   What is the French for wine?   _____

O   What is the French for beer?   _____

TURN BACK FOR THE ANSWERS

MORE RESTAURANT WORDS

THINK OF EACH IMAGE IN YOUR MIND'S EYE FOR ABOUT TEN SECONDS

○ The French for RESTAURANT is   (RESTOROn)
RESTAURANT
Imagine a RESTAURANT at the top of the
Eiffel Tower.

○ The French for KNIFE is COUTEAU   (KOOTOH)
Imagine someone who tries to CUT YOU
with a knife.

○ The French for FORK is FOURCHETTE   (FOORSHET)
Imagine taking a fork and trying to
FORCE IT through a door.

○ The French for SPOON is CUILLER   (KWEE ER)
Imagine a QUEER shaped spoon.

○ The French for MENU is CARTE   (KART)
Imagine a CART loaded to the top with menus.

○ The French for BILL is ADDITION   (ADEESEE OHn)
Imagine practising your ADDITION as
you add up a bill.

○ The French for WAITER is GARÇON   (GARSOHn)
Imagine a waiter who has left the GAS ON,
and burnt your meal.
(N.B. GARÇON is also the word for BOY.)

○ The French for WAITRESS is SERVEUSE   (SERVeZ)
Imagine demanding that the waitress
gives you SERVICE.

○ The French for CUP is TASSE   (TAS)
Imagine a TASSLE hanging from the
handle of a cup.

○ The French for PLATE is ASSIETTE   (ASEE ET)
Imagine looking for a plate and saying
'I SEE IT.'

YOU CAN WRITE YOUR ANSWERS IN, BUT COVER UP THE
RIGHT-HAND PAGE BEFORE GIVING YOUR ANSWERS

O   What is the English for ASSIETTE?
(ASEE ET)   _____

O   What is the English for TASSE? (TAS)   _____

O   What is the English for SERVEUSE?
(SERVeZ)   _____

O   What is the English for GARÇON?
(GARSOHn)   _____

O   What is the English for ADDITION?
(ADEESEE OHn)   _____

O   What is the English for CARTE? (KART)   _____

O   What is the English for CUILLER?
(KWEE ER)   _____

O   What is the English for FOURCHETTE?
(FOORSHET)   _____

O   What is the English for COUTEAU?
(KOOTOH)   _____

O   What is the English for RESTAURANT?
(RESTOROn)   _____

TURN BACK FOR THE ANSWERS

YOU CAN WRITE YOUR ANSWERS IN, BUT COVER UP THE
LEFT-HAND PAGE BEFORE GIVING YOUR ANSWERS

O   What is the French for plate?   _____

O   What is the French for cup?   _____

O   What is the French for waitress?   _____

O   What is the French for waiter?   _____

O   What is the French for bill?   _____

O   What is the French for menu?   _____

O   What is the French for spoon?   _____

O   What is the French for fork?   _____

O   What is the French for knife?   _____

O   What is the French for restaurant?   _____

TURN BACK FOR THE ANSWERS

FAMILY WORDS

THINK OF EACH IMAGE IN YOUR MIND'S EYE FOR ABOUT TEN SECONDS

○ The French for FATHER is PERE   (PER)
Imagine your father eating a PEAR.

○ The French for MOTHER is MERE   (MER)
Imagine your mother mounted on a grey MARE.

○ The French for BROTHER is FRERE   (FRER)
Imagine your brother dressed up as a holy FRIAR.

○ The French for SISTER is SOEUR   (SeR)
Imagine your sister saying 'Hello SIR'.

○ The French for HUSBAND is MARI   (MAREE)
Imagine you MARRY your husband.

○ The French for WIFE is FEMME   (FAM)
Imagine men eating their wives in a FAMine.
(N.B. FEMME is also the word for WOMAN.)

○ The French for SON is FILS   (FEES)
Imagine having to pay school FEES for your son.

○ The French for DAUGHTER is FILLE   (FEE)
Imagine selling your daughter for a FEE.

○ The French for BOY is GARÇON   (GARSOHn)
Imagine a young boy has left the GAS ON.
(N.B. GARÇON is also the word for
WAITER.)

○ The French for GIRL is JEUNE FILLE   (JeN FEE)
Imagine a girl on a YOUNG FILLY.

O   What is the English for JEUNE FILLE?
    (JeN FEE)   _____

O   What is the English for GARÇON?
    (GARSOHn)   _____

O   What is the English for FILLE? (FEE)   _____

O   What is the English for FILS? (FEES)   _____

O   What is the English for FEMME? (FAM)   _____

O   What is the English for MARI? (MAREE)   _____

O   What is the English for SOEUR? (SeR)   _____

O   What is the English for FRERE? (FRER)   _____

O   What is the English for MERE? (MER)   _____

O   What is the English for PERE? (PER)   _____

YOU CAN WRITE YOUR ANSWERS IN

O   What is the French for girl?   _____

O   What is the French for boy?   _____

O   What is the French for daughter?   _____

O   What is the French for son?   _____

O   What is the French for wife?   _____

O   What is the French for husband?   _____

O   What is the French for sister?   _____

O   What is the French for brother?   _____

O   What is the French for mother?   _____

O   What is the French for father?   _____

TURN BACK FOR THE ANSWERS

MORE TRAVELLING WORDS

THINK OF EACH IMAGE IN YOUR MIND'S EYE FOR ABOUT TEN SECONDS

○ The French for GARAGE is GARAGE   (GARAJ)
Imagine a GARAGE under the Eiffel Tower.

○ The French for ROAD is ROUTE   (ROOT)
Imagine roads covered in plant ROOTS.

○ The French for BRIDGE is PONT   (POHn)
Imagine smelling a terrible PONG as you cross a bridge.

○ The French for CAR is AUTO   (OTOH)
Imagine your car has AUTOmatic gears.

○ The French for BOAT is BATEAU   (BATOH)
Imagine going into BATTLE on a boat.

○ The French for OIL is HUILE   (WEEL)
Imagine your WHEEL splashing through a pool of oil.

○ The French for PETROL is ESSENCE   (ESOnS)
Imagine putting vanilla ESSENCE in your petrol.

○ The French for JACK is CRIC   (KREEK)
Imagine being up the CREEK without a jack when you have a puncture.

○ The French for TYRE is PNEU   (PNe)
Imagine needing a NEW tyre.

○ The French for SPANNER is CLEF   (KLAY)
Imagine having a CLAY spanner which falls to bits when you try to use it.
(N.B. CLEF also means KEY.)

31

YOU CAN WRITE YOUR ANSWERS IN, BUT COVER UP THE
RIGHT-HAND PAGE BEFORE GIVING YOUR ANSWERS

○   What is the English for CLEF? (KLAY)   _____

○   What is the English for PNEU? (PNe)   _____

○   What is the English for CRIC? (KREEK)   _____

○   What is the English for ESSENCE?
      (ESOnS)   _____

○   What is the English for HUILE? (WEEL)   _____

○   What is the English for BATEAU?
      (BATOH)   _____

○   What is the English for AUTO? (OTOH)   _____

○   What is the English for PONT? (POHn)   _____

○   What is the English for ROUTE? (ROOT)   _____

○   What is the English for GARAGE?
      (GARAJ)   _____

TURN BACK FOR THE ANSWERS

YOU CAN WRITE YOUR ANSWERS IN, BUT COVER UP THE
LEFT-HAND PAGE BEFORE GIVING YOUR ANSWERS

O   What is the French for spanner?   _____

O   What is the French for tyre?   _____

O   What is the French for jack?   _____

O   What is the French for petrol?   _____

O   What is the French for oil?   _____

O   What is the French for boat?   _____

O   What is the French for car?   _____

O   What is the French for bridge?   _____

O   What is the French for road?   _____

O   What is the French for garage?   _____

TURN BACK FOR THE ANSWERS

AT THE DOCTOR'S

THINK OF EACH IMAGE IN YOUR MIND'S EYE FOR ABOUT TEN SECONDS

○ The French for PAIN is DOULEUR   (DOOLeR)
Imagine being given a DOLLAR to make your
pain go away.

○ The French for ILLNESS is MALADIE   (MALADEE)
Imagine thinking your friend is looking very
ill – he has some MALADY.

○ The French for MOUTH is BOUCHE   (BOOSH)
Imagine a BUSH growing out of your mouth.

○ The French for ARM is BRAS   (BRA)
Imagine a lady's BRA strapped round your arm.

○ The French for LEG is JAMBE   (JOnB)
Imagine JAM spread all over your leg.

○ The French for THROAT is GORGE   (GORJ)
Imagine you GORGE a huge meal which
sticks in your throat.

○ The French for BACK is DOS   (DOH)
Imagine making DOUGH on your mother's back.

○ The French for HAND is MAIN   (MAHn)
Imagine a MAN waving his hand.

○ The French for RIB is COTE   (KOT)
Imagine wrapping a rib in a COAT.

○ The French for TONGUE is LANGUE   (LOnG)
Imagine sticking out a very LONG tongue.

YOU CAN WRITE YOUR ANSWERS IN, BUT COVER UP THE
LEFT-HAND PAGE BEFORE GIVING YOUR ANSWERS

O   What is the English for LANGUE? (LOnG) _____

O   What is the English for COTE? (KOT)   _____

O   What is the English for MAIN? (MAHn)   _____

O   What is the English for DOS? (DOH)   _____

O   What is the English for GORGE? (GORJ)   _____

O   What is the English for JAMBE? (JOnB)   _____

O   What is the English for BRAS? (BRA)   _____

O   What is the English for BOUCHE?
     (BOOSH)   _____

O   What is the English for MALADIE?
     (MALADEE)   _____

O   What is the English for DOULEUR?
     (DOOLeR)   _____

YOU CAN WRITE YOUR ANSWERS IN

○   What is the French for tongue?   _____

○   What is the French for rib?   _____

○   What is the French for hand?   _____

○   What is the French for back?   _____

○   What is the French for throat?   _____

○   What is the French for leg?   _____

○   What is the French for arm?   _____

○   What is the French for mouth?   _____

○   What is the French for illness?   _____

○   What is the French for pain?   _____

TURN BACK FOR THE ANSWERS

NOW TEST YOURSELF

What is the English for   *What is the French for*

1]	LAIT (LAY)	1]	TOMATO
2]	BOISSON (BWASOHn)	2]	GLASS
3]	DOUANE (DWAN)	3]	TOILET
4]	PANTALON (POnTALOHn)	4]	SOCK
5]	AU SECOURS! (OH SKOOR)	5]	DANGER
6]	LIT (LEE)	6]	TABLE
7]	TAPIS (TAPEE)	7]	CURTAIN
8]	VIN (VAHn)	8]	APPLE
9]	ESCARGOT (ESKARGOH)	9]	COFFEE
10]	FOURCHETTE (FOORSHET)	10]	WAITER
11]	TASSE (TAS)	11]	PLATE
12]	MARI (MAREE)	12]	MOTHER
13]	JEUNE FILLE (JeN FEE)	13]	WIFE
14]	CRIC (KREEK)	14]	ROAD
15]	CLEF (KLAY)	15]	BOAT
16]	DOULEUR (DOOLeR)	16]	ILLNESS
17]	BRAS (BRA)	17]	MOUTH
18]	GORGE (GORJ)	18]	TONGUE
19]	FROMAGE (FROMAJ)	19]	BILL
20]	CUILLER (KWEE ER)	20]	GARAGE

Do not worry about the spelling at this stage.

THE ANSWERS ARE ON PAGE 38

THE ANSWERS ARE

1]	MILK	1]	TOMATE
2]	DRINK	2]	VERRE
3]	CUSTOMS	3]	TOILETTES
4]	TROUSERS	4]	CHAUSSETTE
5]	HELP	5]	DANGER
6]	BED	6]	TABLE
7]	CARPET	7]	RIDEAU
8]	WINE	8]	POMME
9]	SNAIL	9]	CAFE
10]	FORK	10]	GARÇON
11]	CUP	11]	ASSIETTE
12]	HUSBAND	12]	MERE
13]	GIRL	13]	FEMME
14]	JACK	14]	ROUTE
15]	SPANNER	15]	BATEAU
16]	PAIN	16]	MALADIE
17]	ARM	17]	BOUCHE
18]	THROAT	18]	LANGUE
19]	CHEESE	19]	ADDITION
20]	SPOON	20]	GARAGE

Since you have now covered 100 words, if your score on this test is over 20/40 you have learned 50 words. If your score is 40/40 you have learned 100 words. Do not worry about spelling errors at this stage of learning.

GENERALLY USEFUL WORDS

THINK OF EACH IMAGE IN YOUR MIND'S EYE FOR ABOUT TEN SECONDS

○ The French for HOUSE is MAISON   (MAYZOHn)
   Imagine a stone-MASON cleaning your house.

○ The French for POLICE is POLICE   (POLEES)
   Imagine the POLICE surrounding the Eiffel Tower.

○ The French for CHEMIST'S SHOP is   (FARMASEE)
   PHARMACIE
   Imagine the PHARMACY in your local chemist's shop.

○ The French for BANK is BANQUE   (BOnK)
   Imagine a BANK at the top of the Eiffel Tower.

○ The French for HOTEL is HOTEL   (OTEL)
   Imagine staying at an HOTEL in the Eiffel Tower.

○ The French for INN is AUBERGE   (OBERJ)
   Imagine piles of AUBERGINES at the
   door of an inn.

○ The French for MARKET is MARCHE   (MARSHAY)
   Imagine MARCHING through a market.

○ The French for BAKER'S SHOP is   (BOOLOnJeREE)
   BOULANGERIE
   Imagine that in France, baker's shops
   sell bread and underwear for
   bulls – BULL LINGERIE. Sometimes
   the bread is wrapped in bull's lingerie.

○ The French for BUTCHER'S SHOP is   (BOOSHeREE)
   BOUCHERIE
   Imagine a BUTCHER'S SHOP beside the Eiffel Tower.

○ The French for STATION is GARE   (GAR)
   Imagine parking your CAR at the station.

YOU CAN WRITE YOUR ANSWERS IN, BUT COVER UP THE RIGHT-HAND PAGE BEFORE GIVING YOUR ANSWERS

○   What is the English for GARE? (GAR)   _____

○   What is the English for BOUCHERIE? (BOOSHeREE)   _____

○   What is the English for BOULANGERIE? (BOOLOnJeREE)   _____

○   What is the English for MARCHE? (MARSHAY)   _____

○   What is the English for AUBERGE? (OBERJ)   _____

○   What is the English for HOTEL? (OTEL)   _____

○   What is the English for BANQUE? (BOnK)   _____

○   What is the English for PHARMACIE? (FARMASEE)   _____

○   What is the English for POLICE? (POLEES)   _____

○   What is the English for MAISON? (MAYZOHn)   _____

TURN BACK FOR THE ANSWERS

O   What is the French for station?   _____

O   What is the French for butcher's shop?   _____

O   What is the French for baker's shop?   _____

O   What is the French for market?   _____

O   What is the French for inn?   _____

O   What is the French for hotel?   _____

O   What is the French for bank?   _____

O   What is the French for chemist's shop?   _____

O   What is the French for police?   _____

O   What is the French for house?   _____

TURN BACK FOR THE ANSWERS

TIME WORDS

THINK OF EACH IMAGE IN YOUR MIND'S EYE FOR ABOUT TEN SECONDS

○ The French for TIME is TEMPS (TOn)
Imagine keeping time with your TONGUE.

○ The French for SECOND is SECONDE (SeGOHnD)
Imagine seeing the Eiffel Tower for a split SECOND.

○ The French for MINUTE is MINUTE (MEENooT)
Imagine it takes you exactly one MINUTE to run to the top of the Eiffel Tower.

○ The French for HOUR is HEURE (eR)
Imagine you meet HER every hour.

○ The French for DAY is JOUR (JOOR)
Imagine not being SURE what day it is.

○ The French for WEEK is SEMAINE (SeMEN)
Imagine getting a SERMON from a priest once a week.

○ The French for MONTH is MOIS (MWA)
Imagine your MA gives you pocket money once a month.

○ The French for YEAR is AN (On)
Imagine thinking 'OH! What a year!'

○ The French for MORNING is MATIN (MATAHn)
Imagine going to a theatre MATINEE in the morning.

○ The French for NIGHT is NUIT (NWEE)
Imagine thinking 'It would be night wheN WE arrived home.'

YOU CAN WRITE YOUR ANSWERS IN, BUT COVER UP THE
LEFT-HAND PAGE BEFORE GIVING YOUR ANSWERS

○   What is the English for NUIT? (NWEE)   _____

○   What is the English for MATIN?
    (MATAHn)   _____

○   What is the English for AN? (On)   _____

○   What is the English for MOIS? (MWA)   _____

○   What is the English for SEMAINE?
    (SeMEN)   _____

○   What is the English for JOUR? (JOOR)   _____

○   What is the English for HEURE? (eR)   _____

○   What is the English for MINUTE?
    (MEENooT)   _____

○   What is the English for SECONDE?
    (SeGOHnD)   _____

○   What is the English for TEMPS? (TOn)   _____

43

YOU CAN WRITE YOUR ANSWERS IN

O   What is the French for night?   _____

O   What is the French for morning?   _____

O   What is the French for year?   _____

O   What is the French for month?   _____

O   What is the French for week?   _____

O   What is the French for day?   _____

O   What is the French for hour?   _____

O   What is the French for minute?   _____

O   What is the French for second?   _____

O   What is the French for time?   _____

TURN BACK FOR THE ANSWERS

QUESTION WORDS

THINK OF EACH IMAGE IN YOUR MIND'S EYE FOR ABOUT TEN SECONDS

O   The French for WHERE is OU   (OO)
     Imagine thinking 'OOH! WHERE are you?'

O   The French for WHY is POURQUOI   (POORKWA)
     Imagine thinking 'WHY is that
     POOR QUACKING duck ill?'

O   The French for HOW is COMMENT   (COMOn)
     Imagine saying 'HOW well you have COME ON.'

O   The French for WHEN is QUAND   (KOn)
     Imagine asking WHEN the CON man called.

O   The French for BECAUSE is PARCE QUE   (PARS Ke)
     Imagine saying you PASSED HER the salt
     BECAUSE she asked for it.

45

YOU CAN WRITE YOUR ANSWERS IN, BUT COVER UP THE
RIGHT-HAND PAGE BEFORE GIVING YOUR ANSWERS

○   What is the English for PARCE QUE?
(PARS Ke)   _____

○   What is the English for QUAND? (KOn)   _____

○   What is the English for COMMENT?
(KOMOn)   _____

○   What is the English for POURQUOI?
(POORKWA)   _____

○   What is the English for OU? (OO)   _____

TURN BACK FOR THE ANSWERS

O   What is the French for because?   _____

O   What is the French for when?   _____

O   What is the French for how?   _____

O   What is the French for why?   _____

O   What is the French for where?   _____

TURN BACK FOR THE ANSWERS

DAYS OF THE WEEK

THINK OF EACH IMAGE IN YOUR MIND'S EYE FOR ABOUT TEN SECONDS

○ The French for SUNDAY is DIMANCHE   (DEEMOnSH)
Imagine someone DEMANDS to see you on Sundays.

○ The French for MONDAY is LUNDI   (LeNDEE)
Imagine your relatives LAND ON you on Mondays.

○ The French for TUESDAY is MARDI   (MARDEE)
Imagine MARDI GRAS, the carnival,
always takes place on Tuesdays.

○ The French for WEDNESDAY is   (MERKReDEE)
MERCREDI
Imagine Wednesday is MARKET DAY.

○ The French for THURSDAY is JEUDI   (JeDEE)
Imagine you were sold SHODDY goods last Thursday.

○ The French for FRIDAY is VENDREDI   (VOnDReDEE)
Imagine Friday is the day you go for a little
WANDER IN town.

○ The French for SATURDAY is SAMEDI   (SAMDEE)
Imagine Saturdays always seem the same to
you SOMEDAYS.

YOU CAN WRITE YOUR ANSWERS IN, BUT COVER UP THE
LEFT-HAND PAGE BEFORE GIVING YOUR ANSWERS

O   What is the English for SAMEDI?
     (SAMDEE)   _____

O   What is the English for VENDREDI?
     (VOnDReDEE)   _____

O   What is the English for JEUDI? (JeDEE)   _____

O   What is the English for MERCREDI?
     (MERKReDEE)   _____

O   What is the English for MARDI?
     (MARDEE)   _____

O   What is the English for LUNDI? (LeNDEE)   _____

O   What is the English for DIMANCHE?
     (DEEMOnSH)   _____

YOU CAN WRITE YOUR ANSWERS IN

O   What is the French for Saturday?   _____

O   What is the French for Friday?   _____

O   What is the French for Thursday?   _____

O   What is the French for Wednesday?   _____

O   What is the French for Tuesday?   _____

O   What is the French for Monday?   _____

O   What is the French for Sunday?   _____

TURN BACK FOR THE ANSWERS

HOUSE WORDS

THINK OF EACH IMAGE IN YOUR MIND'S EYE FOR ABOUT TEN SECONDS

○ The French for DOOR is PORTE   (PORT)
Imagine a PORT with a huge door at the entrance.

○ The French for WINDOW is FENETRE   (FeNETR)
Imagine covering windows with a FINE NET.

○ The French for GARDEN is JARDIN   (JARDAHn)
Imagine a GARDEN on the top of the Eiffel Tower.

○ The French for ROOF is TOIT   (TWA)
Imagine a TWANging noise on the roof.

○ The French for CEILING is PLAFOND   (PLAFOHn)
Imagine using a PLATFORM to paint the ceiling.

○ The French for STAIRCASE is ESCALIER   (ESKALEE AY)
Imagine your staircase is like an ESCALATOR.

○ The French for FLOOR is PLANCHER   (PLOnSHAY)
Imagine PLUNGING through rotten floors.

○ The French for WALL is MUR   (MooR)
Imagine a MURAL painted on your wall.

○ The French for KITCHEN is CUISINE   (KWEEZEEN)
Imagine preparing beautiful CUISINE in your kitchen.

○ The French for ROOM is PIECE   (PEE ES)
Imagine someone writing to you to say 'P.S. Your room will be very small.'

51

YOU CAN WRITE YOUR ANSWERS IN, BUT COVER UP THE
RIGHT-HAND PAGE BEFORE GIVING YOUR ANSWERS

○   What is the English for PIECE? (PEE ES) _____

○   What is the English for CUISINE?
    (KWEEZEEN)   _____

○   What is the English for MUR? (MooR)   _____

○   What is the English for PLANCHER?
    (PLOnSHAY)   _____

○   What is the English for ESCALIER?
    (ESKALEE AY)   _____

○   What is the English for PLAFOND?
    (PLAFOHn)   _____

○   What is the English for TOIT? (TWA)   _____

○   What is the English for JARDIN?
    (JARDAHn)   _____

○   What is the English for FENETRE?
    (FeNETR)   _____

○   What is the English for PORTE? (PORT)   _____

TURN BACK FOR THE ANSWERS

YOU CAN WRITE YOUR ANSWERS IN, BUT COVER UP THE
LEFT-HAND PAGE BEFORE GIVING YOUR ANSWERS

○   What is the French for room?   _____

○   What is the French for kitchen?   _____

○   What is the French for wall?   _____

○   What is the French for floor?   _____

○   What is the French for stairs?   _____

○   What is the French for ceiling?   _____

○   What is the French for roof?   _____

○   What is the French for garden?   _____

○   What is the French for window?   _____

○   What is the French for door?   _____

TURN BACK FOR THE ANSWERS

NUMBERS

THINK OF EACH IMAGE IN YOUR MIND'S EYE FOR ABOUT TEN SECONDS

O The French for ONE is UN   (en)
Imagine eating ONE ONion.

O The French for TWO is DEUX   (De)
Imagine thinking 'TWO will DO.'

O The French for THREE is TROIS   (TRWA)
Imagine you TRY to say trois THREE times.

O The French for FOUR is QUATRE   (KATR)
Imagine looking at FOUR CATS.

O The French for FIVE is CINQ   (SAHnK)
Imagine watching as FIVE ships SANK.

O The French for SIX is SIX   (SEES)
Imagine telling someone to CEASE saying
'SIX times SIX'.

O The French for SEVEN is SEPT   (SET)
Imagine you SET your alarm for SEVEN o'clock.

O The French for EIGHT is HUIT   (WEET)
Imagine EIGHT sheaves of WHEAT.

O The French for NINE is NEUF   (NeF)
Imagine saying 'ENOUGH is enough. I'm going
to dial 999.'

O The French for ZERO is ZERO   (ZAYROH)
Imagine meeting someone at the Eiffel Tower at
ZERO hour.

YOU CAN WRITE YOUR ANSWERS IN, BUT COVER UP THE
LEFT-HAND PAGE BEFORE GIVING YOUR ANSWERS

○   What is the English for ZERO? (ZAYROH) _____

○   What is the English for NEUF? (NeF)   _____

○   What is the English for HUIT? (WEET)   _____

○   What is the English for SEPT? (SET)   _____

○   What is the English for SIX? (SEES)   _____

○   What is the English for CINQ? (SAHnK)   _____

○   What is the English for QUATRE? (KATR) _____

○   What is the English for TROIS? (TRWA)   _____

○   What is the English for DEUX? (De)   _____

○   What is the English for UN? (en)   _____

YOU CAN WRITE YOUR ANSWERS IN

O   What is the French for zero?   _____

O   What is the French for nine?   _____

O   What is the French for eight?   _____

O   What is the French for seven?   _____

O   What is the French for six?   _____

O   What is the French for five?   _____

O   What is the French for four?   _____

O   What is the French for three?   _____

O   What is the French for two?   _____

O   What is the French for one?   _____

TURN BACK FOR THE ANSWERS

GENERALLY USEFUL WORDS

THINK OF EACH IMAGE IN YOUR MIND'S EYE FOR ABOUT TEN SECONDS

○ The French for VERY is TRES   (TRAY)
Imagine a TRAY VERY full.

○ The French for SOON is BIENTOT   (BEE AHnTOH)
Imagine thinking 'I will have BEEN TO
that place SOON.'

○ The French for HERE is ICI   (EESEE)
Imagine thinking 'It is very EASY HERE
to learn French.'

○ The French for THERE is LA   (LA)
Imagine thinking 'I might get some ooh
LA LA there!'

○ The French for QUITE is ASSEZ   (ASAY)
Imagine thinking 'I SAY, he is QUITE clever.'

○ The French for EASY is FACILE   (FASEEL)
Imagine thinking 'He has an EASY but
FACILE manner.'

○ The French for DIFFICULT is   (DEEFEESEEL)
DIFFICILE
Imagine it is DIFFICULT to climb the
Eiffel Tower.

○ The French for GOOD is BON   (BOHn)
Imagine eating GOOD BON bons – bon
bons are goody goodies.

YOU CAN WRITE YOUR ANSWERS IN, BUT COVER UP THE
RIGHT-HAND PAGE BEFORE GIVING YOUR ANSWERS

O   What is the English for BON? (BOHn)   _____

O   What is the English for DIFFICILE?
    (DEEFEESEEL)   _____

O   What is the English for FACILE?
    (FASEEL)   _____

O   What is the English for ASSEZ? (ASAY)   _____

O   What is the English for LA? (LA)   _____

O   What is the English for ICI? (EESEE)   _____

O   What is the English for BIENTOT?
    (BEE AHnTOH)   _____

O   What is the English for TRES? (TRAY)   _____

TURN BACK FOR THE ANSWERS

YOU CAN WRITE YOUR ANSWERS IN, BUT COVER UP THE
LEFT-HAND PAGE BEFORE GIVING YOUR ANSWERS

O   What is the French for very?   _____

O   What is the French for soon?   _____

O   What is the French for here?   _____

O   What is the French for there?   _____

O   What is the French for quite?   _____

O   What is the French for easy?   _____

O   What is the French for difficult?   _____

O   What is the French for good?   _____

TURN BACK FOR THE ANSWERS

ON THE BEACH AND LEISURE

THINK OF EACH IMAGE IN YOUR MIND'S EYE FOR ABOUT TEN SECONDS

O   The French for BEACH is PLAGE   (PLAJ)
    Imagine a PLAQUE on a Normandy beach,
    to commemorate the fighting.

O   The French for SEA is MER   (MER)
    Imagine a MARE and her foal plunging into the sea.

O   The French for SUN is SOLEIL   (SOLAY)
    Imagine it being very hot in the sun,
    SO LAY down and get a suntan.

O   The French for SAND is SABLE   (SABL)
    Imagine a SABLE skin coat, with sand on it.

O   The French for TOWEL is SERVIETTE   (SERVEE ET)
    Imagine using a SERVIETTE as a towel.

O   The French for PICNIC is PIQUE-NIQUE   (PEEK-NEEK)
    Imagine taking a PICNIC to the Eiffel Tower.

O   The French for RIVER is RIVIERE   (REEVEE ER)
    Imagine a river flowing down to the RIVIERA.

O   The French for FOREST is FORET   (FORAY)
    Imagine going on a FORAY into the forest.

O   The French for COUNTRYSIDE is   (COnPANYe)
    CAMPAGNE
    Imagine going with a COMPANION into the
    countryside.

O   The French for MOUNTAIN is   (MOHnTANYe)
     MONTAGNE
    Imagine the Eiffel Tower on top of a MOUNTAIN.

○　What is the English for MONTAGNE?
　　(MOHnTANYe)　　　　　　　　　＿＿＿＿＿＿＿

○　What is the English for CAMPAGNE?
　　(COnPANYe)　　　　　　　　　　＿＿＿＿＿＿＿

○　What is the English for FORET?
　　(FORAY)　　　　　　　　　　　　＿＿＿＿＿＿＿

○　What is the English for RIVIERE?
　　(REEVEE ER)　　　　　　　　　　＿＿＿＿＿＿＿

○　What is the English for PIQUE-NIQUE?
　　(PEEK-NEEK)　　　　　　　　　　＿＿＿＿＿＿＿

○　What is the English for SERVIETTE?
　　(SERVEE ET)　　　　　　　　　　＿＿＿＿＿＿＿

○　What is the English for SABLE? (SABL)　＿＿＿＿＿＿＿

○　What is the English for SOLEIL? (SOLAY) ＿＿＿＿＿＿＿

○　What is the English for MER? (MER)　　＿＿＿＿＿＿＿

○　What is the English for PLAGE? (PLAJ)　＿＿＿＿＿＿＿

YOU CAN WRITE YOUR ANSWERS IN

O   What is the French for mountain?   _____

O   What is the French for countryside?   _____

O   What is the French for forest?   _____

O   What is the French for river?   _____

O   What is the French for picnic?   _____

O   What is the French for towel?   _____

O   What is the French for sand?   _____

O   What is the French for sun?   _____

O   What is the French for sea?   _____

O   What is the French for beach?   _____

TURN BACK FOR THE ANSWERS

COLOURS

THINK OF EACH IMAGE IN YOUR MIND'S EYE FOR ABOUT TEN SECONDS

○ The French for BLACK is NOIR   (NWAR)
Imagine someone telling you 'There is NO "R" in black.'

○ The French for WHITE is BLANC   (BLOn)
Imagine a BLONDE, white-haired girl.

○ The French for RED is ROUGE   (ROOJ)
Imagine someone whose face is reddened with ROUGE.

○ The French for YELLOW is JAUNE   (JON)
Imagine someone yellow from JAUNDICE.

○ The French for GREEN is VERT   (VER)
Imagine someone with a VERY green face.

○ The French for BLUE is BLEU   (BLe)
Imagine painting the Eiffel Tower blue.

○ The French for PINK is ROSE   (ROZ)
Imagine a pink ROSE.

○ The French for ORANGE is ORANGE   (OROnJ)
Imagine painting the Eiffel Tower a bright orange.

○ The French for GOLD(en) is DORE   (DORAY)
Imagine a gold DOOR.

○ The French for GREY is GRIS   (GREE)
Imagine grey coloured GREASE.

YOU CAN WRITE YOUR ANSWERS IN, BUT COVER UP THE
RIGHT-HAND PAGE BEFORE GIVING YOUR ANSWERS

O   What is the English for GRIS? (GREE)   _____

O   What is the English for DORE? (DORAY)   _____

O   What is the English for ORANGE?
(OROnJ)   _____

O   What is the English for ROSE? (ROZ)   _____

O   What is the English for BLEU? (BLe)   _____

O   What is the English for VERT? (VER)   _____

O   What is the English for JAUNE? (JON)   _____

O   What is the English for ROUGE? (ROOJ)   _____

O   What is the English for BLANC? (BLOn)   _____

O   What is the English for NOIR? (NWAR)   _____

TURN BACK FOR THE ANSWERS

YOU CAN WRITE YOUR ANSWERS IN, BUT COVER UP THE
LEFT-HAND PAGE BEFORE GIVING YOUR ANSWERS

O   What is the French for grey?   _____

O   What is the French for gold(en)?   _____

O   What is the French for orange?   _____

O   What is the French for pink?   _____

O   What is the French for blue?   _____

O   What is the French for green?   _____

O   What is the French for yellow?   _____

O   What is the French for red?   _____

O   What is the French for white?   _____

O   What is the French for black?   _____

TURN BACK FOR THE ANSWERS

GENERALLY USEFUL WORDS

THINK OF EACH IMAGE IN YOUR MIND'S EYE FOR ABOUT TEN SECONDS

○ The French for ENGAGED is OCCUPE   (OKooPAY)
Imagine a toilet being ENGAGED
because someone is OCCUPYING it.

○ The French for CLOSED is FERME   (FERMAY)
Imagine something being CLOSED FOR ME.

○ The French for PLEASE is
S'IL VOUS PLAIT   (SEEL VOO PLAY)
Imagine saying 'PLEASE can I have a
SILVER PLATE.'

○ The French for THANK YOU is MERCI   (MERSEE)
Imagine THANKING someone for the
MERCY he has shown you.

○ The French for OPEN is OUVERT   (OOVER)
Imagine shops OPEN OVER Christmas.

YOU CAN WRITE YOUR ANSWERS IN, BUT COVER UP THE
LEFT-HAND PAGE BEFORE GIVING YOUR ANSWERS

O   What is the English for MERCI?
     (MERSEE)   _____

O   What is the English for S'IL VOUS PLAIT?
     (SEEL VOO PLAY)   _____

O   What is the English for FERME?
     (FERMAY)   _____

O   What is the English for OCCUPE?
     (OKooPAY)   _____

O   What is the English for OUVERT?
     (OOVER)   _____

YOU CAN WRITE YOUR ANSWERS IN

O   What is the French for thank you?   _____

O   What is the French for please?   _____

O   What is the French for closed?   _____

O   What is the French for engaged?   _____

O   What is the French for open?   _____

TURN BACK FOR THE ANSWERS

MORE FOOD WORDS

THINK OF EACH IMAGE IN YOUR MIND'S EYE FOR ABOUT TEN SECONDS

○ The French for RICE is RIZ   (REE)
   Imagine you RAISE rice.

○ The French for CHICKEN is POULET   (POOLAY)
   Imagine a chicken hanging from a PULLEY.

○ The French for SALT is SEL   (SEL)
   Imagine you SELL salt.

○ The French for SAUCE is SAUCE   (SOS)
   Imagine you pour SAUCE from the top of
   the Eiffel Tower.

○ The French for SUGAR is SUCRE   (SooKR)
   Imagine you are a SUCKER for sugar.

YOU CAN WRITE YOUR ANSWERS IN, BUT COVER UP THE
RIGHT-HAND PAGE BEFORE GIVING YOUR ANSWERS

O   What is the English for SUCRE?
     (SooKR)   _____

O   What is the English for SAUCE?
     (SOS)   _____

O   What is the English for SEL?
     (SEL)   _____

O   What is the English for POULET?
     (POOLAY)   _____

O   What is the English for RIZ?
     (REE)   _____

TURN BACK FOR THE ANSWERS

O   What is the French for sugar?   _____

O   What is the French for sauce?   _____

O   What is the French for salt?   _____

O   What is the French for chicken?   _____

O   What is the French for rice?   _____

TURN BACK FOR THE ANSWERS

SOME USEFUL VERBS

THINK OF EACH IMAGE IN YOUR MIND'S EYE FOR ABOUT TEN SECONDS

○ The French for I AM is JE SUIS   (Je SWEE)
    Imagine I AM a SWEDE.

○ The French for I SEE is JE VOIS   (Je VWA)
    Imagine I SEE FAR.

○ The French for I WANT is JE VEUX   (Je Ve)
    Imagine I WANT your FUR for something.

○ The French for I EAT is JE MANGE   (Je MOnJ)
    Imagine I EAT blancMANGE.

○ The French for I HAVE is J'AI   (JAY)
    Imagine I HAVE been JAY walking.

○ The French for YOU ARE is VOUS ETES   (VOOZ ET)
    Imagine someone saying WHO SAID YOU ARE here.

○ The French for YOU SEE is VOUS   (VOO VWA YAY)
    VOYEZ
    Imagine someone shouting 'I'll SEE YOU
    on a VOYAGE.'

○ The French for YOU WANT is VOUS   (VOO VOOLAY)
    VOULEZ
    Imagine YOU WANT a WOOLLEN jumper.

○ The French for YOU HAVE is VOUS AVEZ   (VOOZ AVAY)
    Imagine YOU HAVE given something AWAY.

○ The French for YOU EAT is VOUS   (VOO MOnJAY)
    MANGEZ
    Imagine YOU EAT a MANGY cat.

YOU CAN WRITE YOUR ANSWERS IN, BUT COVER UP THE
LEFT-HAND PAGE BEFORE GIVING YOUR ANSWERS

○   What is the English for VOUS MANGEZ?
    (VOO MOnJAY)   _____

○   What is the English for VOUS AVEZ?
    (VOOZ AVAY)   _____

○   What is the English for VOUS VOULEZ?
    (VOO VOOLAY)   _____

○   What is the English for VOUS VOYEZ?
    (VOO VWA YAY)   _____

○   What is the English for VOUS ETES?
    (VOOZ ET)   _____

○   What is the English for J'AI? (JAY)   _____

○   What is the English for JE MANGE?
    (Je MOnJ)   _____

○   What is the English for JE VEUX? (Je Ve) _____

○   What is the English for JE VOIS?
    (Je VWA)   _____

○   What is the English for JE SUIS?
    (Je SWEE)   _____

73

YOU CAN WRITE YOUR ANSWERS IN

O   What is the French for I am?   _____

O   What is the French for I see?   _____

O   What is the French for I want?   _____

O   What is the French for I eat?   _____

O   What is the French for I have?   _____

O   What is the French for you are?   _____

O   What is the French for you see?   _____

O   What is the French for you want?   _____

O   What is the French for you have?   _____

O   What is the French for you eat?   _____

TURN BACK FOR THE ANSWERS

A FINAL TEST

What is the English for   *What is the French for*

1]	PAIN (PAHn)	1]	EGG ....
2]	NAPPE (NAP)	2]	CUTLERY ....
3]	BILLET (BEE AY)	3]	PASSPORT ....
4]	ARGENT (ARJOn)	4]	JACKET ....
5]	JUPE (JooP)	5]	AMBULANCE ....
6]	DENTISTE (DOn TEEST)	6]	CLOCK ....
7]	ARMOIRE (ARMWAR)	7]	PEAR ....
8]	CHAMPIGNON .... (SHOn PEENYOHn)	8]	KNIFE ....
9]	CARTE (KART)	9]	BROTHER ....
10]	ESSENCE (ESOnS)	10]	TYRE ....
11]	JAMBE (JOnB)	11]	BACK ....
12]	MAISON (MAYZOHn)	12]	BAKER'S SHOP ....
13]	JOUR (JOOR)	13]	MORNING ....
14]	POURQUOI (POORKWA)	14]	WHERE ....
15]	LUNDI (LeNDEE)	15]	DOOR ....
16]	MARDI (MARDEE)	16]	WINDOW ....
17]	PIECE (PEE ES)	17]	NINE ....
18]	DEUX (De)	18]	HERE ....
19]	TRES (TRAY)	19]	THERE ....
20]	MER (MER)	20]	TOWEL ....
21]	SOLEIL (SOLAY)	21]	WHITE ....
22]	ROUGE (ROOJ)	22]	PINK ....
23]	MERCI (MERSEE)	23]	CLOSED ....
24]	SEL (SEL)	24]	SUGAR ....
25]	JE SUIS (Je SWEE)	25]	I HAVE ....
26]	VOUS VOULEZ .... (VOO VOOLAY)	26]	YOU SEE ....
27]	ESCARGOT (ESKARGOH)	27]	CHAIR ....
28]	AUBERGE (OBERJ)	28]	BOY ....
29]	GRIS (GREE)	29]	POLICE ....
30]	PLACARD (PLAKAR)	30]	MONTH ....

THE ANSWERS ARE ON PAGE 76

THE ANSWERS ARE

1]	BREAD	1]	OEUF
2]	TABLECLOTH	2]	COUVERT
3]	TICKET	3]	PASSEPORT
4]	MONEY	4]	VESTE
5]	SKIRT	5]	AMBULANCE
6]	DENTIST	6]	PENDULE
7]	WARDROBE	7]	POIRE
8]	MUSHROOM	8]	COUTEAU
9]	MENU	9]	FRERE
10]	PETROL	10]	PNEU
11]	LEG	11]	DOS
12]	HOUSE	12]	BOULANGERIE
13]	DAY	13]	MATIN
14]	WHY	14]	OU
15]	MONDAY	15]	PORTE
16]	TUESDAY	16]	FENETRE
17]	ROOM	17]	NEUF
18]	TWO	18]	ICI
19]	VERY	19]	LA
20]	SEA	20]	SERVIETTE
21]	SUN	21]	BLANC
22]	RED	22]	ROSE
23]	THANKS	23]	FERME
24]	SALT	24]	SUCRE
25]	I AM	25]	J'AI
26]	YOU WANT	26]	VOUS VOYEZ
27]	SNAIL	27]	CHAISE
28]	INN	28]	GARÇON
29]	GREY	29]	POLICE
30]	CUPBOARD	30]	MOIS

Do not worry about spelling. If you had more than 30/60 correct you have learned 100+ words. 45/60 = 150 words and so on.

IMPORTANT NOTE

This is the end of the course. We hope you have enjoyed it. Of course what you have learned will not make you fluent, but it will help enormously in a large number of situations which you will meet abroad. Don't be afraid to try out what you have learned. Your host will appreciate you making the effort, even if you are sometimes wrong.

The Linkword Method is a very fast method of learning. However, as with any other method of language learning, some of the words will be forgotten unless you go over them from time to time or use them in real life situations. It is strongly recommended that you go over the whole course again a day or two after you have completed it, and then about a month later. Don't worry about forgetting some words. You will be surprised at how quickly you relearn any that you have forgotten when you go over the course again, and just think of all the words you *have* learned.

GLOSSARY

AMBULANCE	– AMBULANCE	CUSTOMS	– DOUANE
APPLE	– POMME	CUTLERY	– COUVERT
ARM	– BRAS	DANGER	– DANGER
ARMCHAIR	– FAUTEUIL	DAUGHTER	– FILLE
BACK	– DOS	DAY	– JOUR
BAKER'S SHOP	– BOULANGERIE	DENTIST	– DENTISTE
BANK	– BANQUE	DIFFICULT	– DIFFICILE
BEACH	– PLAGE	DINNER	– DÎNER
BECAUSE	– PARCE QUE	DOCTOR	– MÉDECIN
BED	– LIT	DOOR	– PORTE
BEER	– BIÈRE	DRESS	– ROBE
BILL	– ADDITION	DRINK	– BOISSON
BLACK	– NOIR	EASY	– FACILE
BLUE	– BLEU	EGG	– OEUF
BOAT	– BATEAU	ENGAGED	– OCCUPÉ
BOY	– GARÇON	ENTRANCE	– ENTRÉE
BREAD	– PAIN	EXIT	– SORTIE
BRIDGE	– PONT	FATHER	– PÈRE
BROTHER	– FRÈRE	FIRE!	– AU FEU!
BUTCHER'S SHOP	– BOUCHERIE	FLOOR	– PLANCHER
BUTTER	– BEURRE	FOOD	– NOURRITURE
CABBAGE	– CHOU	FOREST	– FORÊT
CAR	– AUTO	FORK	– FOURCHETTE
CARPET	– TAPIS	GARAGE	– GARAGE
CEILING	– PLAFOND	GARDEN	– JARDIN
CHAIR	– CHAISE	GARLIC	– AÏL
CHEESE	– FROMAGE	GIRL	– JEUNE FILLE
CHEMIST'S SHOP	– PHARMACIE	GLASS	– VERRE
CHICKEN	– POULET	GOLD(en)	– DORÉ
CLOCK	– PENDULE	GOOD	– BON
CLOSED	– FERMÉ	GREEN	– VERT
COFFEE	– CAFÉ	GREY	– GRIS
COUNTRYSIDE	– CAMPAGNE	HAND	– MAIN
CUP	– TASSE	HAT	– CHAPEAU
CUPBOARD	– PLACARD	HELP!	– AU SECOURS!
CURTAIN	– RIDEAU	HERE	– ICI

HOSPITAL	– HÔPITAL	PLEASE	– S'IL VOUS PLAÎT
HOTEL	– HÔTEL	POLICE	– POLICE
HOUR	– HEURE	POTATO	– POMME DE TERRE
HOUSE	– MAISON	QUITE	– ASSEZ
HOW	– COMMENT	RED	– ROUGE
HUSBAND	– MARI	RIB	– CÔTE
ILLNESS	– MALADIE	RICE	– RIZ
INN	– AUBERGE	RIVER	– RIVIÈRE
JACK	– CRIC	ROAD	– ROUTE
JACKET	– VESTE	ROOF	– TOIT
KITCHEN	– CUISINE	ROOM	– PIÈCE
KNIFE	– COUTEAU	SALT	– SEL
LEG	– JAMBE	SAND	– SABLE
MARKET	– MARCHÉ	SAUCE	– SAUCE
MEAT	– VIANDE	SEA	– MER
MENU	– CARTE	SECOND	– SECONDE
MILK	– LAIT	SHOE	– CHAUSSURE
MINUTE	– MINUTE	SISTER	– SOEUR
MONEY	– ARGENT	SKIRT	– JUPE
MONTH	– MOIS	SNAIL	– ESCARGOT
MORNING	– MATIN	RESTAURANT	– RESTAURANT
MOTHER	– MÈRE	SOCK	– CHAUSSETTE
MOUNTAIN	– MONTAGNE	SON	– FILS
MOUTH	– BOUCHE	SOON	– BIENTÔT
MUSHROOM	– CHAMPIGNON	SPANNER	– CLEF
NIGHT	– NUIT	SPOON	– CUILLER
WHERE	– OÙ	STAIRCASE	– ESCALIER
OIL	– HUILE	STATION	– GARE
OPEN	– OUVERT	SUGAR	– SUCRE
ORANGE	– ORANGE	SUITCASE	– VALISE
PAIN	– DOULEUR	SUN	– SOLEIL
PASSPORT	– PASSEPORT	TABLE	– TABLE
PEACH	– PÊCHE	TABLECLOTH	– NAPPE
PEAR	– POIRE	TELEPHONE	– TÉLÉPHONE
PETROL	– ESSENCE	THANK YOU	– MERCI
PIANO	– PIANO	THERE	– LÀ
PICNIC	– PIQUE-NIQUE	THROAT	– GORGE
PINK	– ROSE	TICKET	– BILLET
PLATE	– ASSIETTE	TIME	– TEMPS

TIP	– POURBOIRE
TOILET	– TOILETTES
TOMATO	– TOMATE
TONGUE	– LANGUE
TOWEL	– SERVIETTE
TROUSERS	– PANTALON
TYRE	– PNEU
UNDERPANTS	– SLIP
VERY	– TRÈS
WAITER	– GARÇON
WAITRESS	– SERVEUSE
WALL	– MUR
WARDROBE	– ARMOIRE
WATER	– EAU
WEEK	– SEMAINE
WHEN	– QUAND
WHITE	– BLANC
WHY	– POURQUOI
WIFE	– FEMME
WINDOW	– FENÊTRE
WINE	– VIN
YEAR	– AN
YELLOW	– JAUNE
YOU ARE	– VOUS ÊTES
YOU EAT	– VOUS MANGEZ
YOU HAVE	– VOUS AVEZ
YOU SEE	– VOUS VOYEZ
YOU WANT	– VOUS VOULEZ
I AM	– JE SUIS
I EAT	– JE MANGE
I HAVE	– J'AI
I SEE	– JE VOIS
I WANT	– JE VEUX

Days of the Week

MONDAY	– LUNDI
TUESDAY	– MARDI
WEDNESDAY	– MERCREDI
THURSDAY	– JEUDI
FRIDAY	– VENDREDI
SATURDAY	– SAMEDI
SUNDAY	– DIMANCHE

Numbers

ONE	– UN
TWO	– DEUX
THREE	– TROIS
FOUR	– QUATRE
FIVE	– CINQ
SIX	– SIX
SEVEN	– SEPT
EIGHT	– HUIT
NINE	– NEUF
ZERO	– ZÉRO

LINKWORD FRENCH
by Dr Michael M. Gruneberg

LINKWORD is the language course which teaches you how to remember what you learn as you learn it.

LINKWORD FRENCH is an ideal follow-up to **LINKWORD FRENCH IN A DAY**. In addition to refreshing most of the vocabulary you have already learned, **LINKWORD FRENCH** teaches you an additional extensive vocabulary using the same Linkword method. Furthermore, the **LINKWORD FRENCH** book links the words taught to grammar points in a simple step by step way, and both grammar and vocabulary learning is reinforced by translation exercises which have been carefully designed to maximize speed of learning. After 10–12 hours you will not only have an extensive vocabulary, but the ability to construct sentences using the grammar.

'The most entertaining language system of all: it works and it's fun'
Guardian

LINKWORD works by association and memory to teach vocabulary <u>and</u> <u>grammar</u> in a simple step by step way. If you are a business person or holidaymaker and want to take your French to a higher level, if you are studying French at school or if you learned French at school and are now rusty – whatever your reasons – **LINKWORD FRENCH** will help you improve fast and cope more confidently.

0 552 13053 2

LINKWORD
LANGUAGE SYSTEM
by Dr Michael M. Gruneberg

LINKWORD is the language course which teaches you how to remember what you learn as you learn it. LINKWORD is the fastest, the easiest, the most enjoyable way to learn a language and is ideal for holidays, business travel and schoolwork!

FOR DETAILS OF HOW TO ORDER AND MORE INFORMATION ABOUT LINKWORD TURN OVER THIS PAGE

LINKWORD LANGUAGE SYSTEM BOOKS, AUDIO TAPES AND BOOK AND TAPE PACKS AVAILABLE FROM CORGI BOOKS

THE PRICES SHOWN BELOW WERE CORRECT AT THE TIME OF GOING TO PRESS. HOWEVER TRANSWORLD PUBLISHERS RESERVE THE RIGHT TO SHOW NEW RETAIL PRICES ON COVERS WHICH MAY DIFFER FROM THOSE PREVIOUSLY ADVERTISED IN THE TEXT OR ELSEWHERE.

☐	14246 8	LINKWORD FRENCH IN A DAY	£3.99
☐	13053 2	LINKWORD LANGUAGE COURSE: FRENCH	£4.99
☐	13916 5	LINKWORD LANGUAGE COURSE: FURTHER FRENCH	£4.99
☐	13054 0	LINKWORD LANGUAGE COURSE: GERMAN	£4.99
☐	14247 6	LINKWORD SPANISH IN A DAY	£3.99
☐	13055 9	LINKWORD LANGUAGE COURSE: SPANISH	£4.99
☐	13056 7	LINKWORD LANGUAGE COURSE: ITALIAN	£4.99
☐	13907 6	LINKWORD LANGUAGE COURSE: GREEK	£4.99
☐	13906 8	LINKWORD LANGUAGE COURSE: PORTUGUESE	£4.99
☐	13225 X	LINKWORD AUDIO TAPE: FRENCH	£6.95*
☐	14062 7	LINKWORD AUDIO TAPE: FURTHER FRENCH	£6.95*
☐	13226 8	LINKWORD AUDIO TAPE: GERMAN	£6.95*
☐	13227 6	LINKWORD AUDIO TAPE: SPANISH	£6.95*
☐	13228 4	LINKWORD AUDIO TAPE: ITALIAN	£6.95*
☐	13955 6	LINKWORD AUDIO TAPE: GREEK	£6.95*
☐	13966 1	LINKWORD AUDIO TAPE: PORTUGUESE	£6.95*
☐	00500 2	LINKWORD BOOK AND TAPE PACK: FRENCH	£11.99*
☐	00370 0	LINKWORD BOOK AND TAPE PACK: GERMAN	£11.99*
☐	00501 0	LINKWORD BOOK AND TAPE PACK: SPANISH	£11.99*

*inclusive of VAT

All Corgi/Bantam Books are available at your bookshop or newsagent, or can be ordered from the following address:
Corgi/Bantam Books
Cash Sales Department
PO Box 11, Falmouth, Cornwall TR10 9EN
UK and BFPO customers please send a cheque or postal order (no currency) and allow £1.00 for postage and packing for the first book plus 50p for the second book and 30p for each additional book to a maximum charge of £3.00 (7 books plus).
Overseas customers, including Eire, please allow £2.00 for postage and packing for the first book plus £1.00 for the second book and 50p for each subsequent title ordered.

NAME (Block letters) ....

ADDRESS ....

....